THE NIGHTLIFE

ALSO BY ELISE PASCHEN

POETRY
Houses: Coasts
Infidelities
Bestiary

CO-EDITOR
Poetry in Motion
Poetry in Motion from Coast to Coast
Poetry Speaks
Poetry Speaks Expanded

EDITOR
Poetry Speaks to Children
Poetry Speaks Who I Am

the NIGHTLIFE

POEMS BY

Elise Paschen

 Red Hen Press | *Pasadena, CA*

Book layout by Selena Trager

Library of Congress Cataloging-in-Publication Data

Names: Paschen, Elise, author.
Title: The nightlife / poems by Elise Paschen.
Description: First edition. | Pasadena, Ca : Red Hen Press, [2017].
Identifiers: LCCN 2016048405 | ISBN 9781597090278 (pbk. : alk. paper)
Classification: LCC PS3566.A77283 A6 2017 | DDC 811/.54—dc23
LC record available at https://lccn.loc.gov/2016048405

The National Endowment for the Arts, the Los Angeles County Arts Commission,
the Dwight Stuart Youth Fund, the Max Factor Family Foundation, the Pasadena
Tournament of Roses Foundation, the Pasadena Arts & Culture Commission and the
City of Pasadena Cultural Affairs Division, the City of Los Angeles Department of
Cultural Affairs, the Audrey & Sydney Irmas Charitable Foundation, Sony Pictures
Entertainment, Amazon Literary Partnership, and the Sherwood Foundation partially
support Red Hen Press.

First Edition
Published by Red Hen Press
www.redhen.org

ACKNOWLEDGMENTS

Grateful acknowledgment is made to the editors of the following publications:

The Academy of American Poets *Poem-a-Day*: "After the Squall" and "Division Street"; *Fifth Wednesday*: "Falls," "Haiku," "High Ground," "Of Mice," "Seed," "Skein," and "text"; *Harvard Review*: "The Marriage Bed"; *Hopkins Review*: "High-Rise"; *Hudson Review*: "My Mother Descends"; *New Criterion*: "Impromptu"; *The New Yorker*: "The Wide Stars Above Our Sky*"; *Poetry Magazine*: "Ghost, Fountain," "Hedgerows," "Lear's Wife," and *"The Tree Agreement"*; *TAB: A Journal of Poetry & Poetics*: "Accidents" and "Closing House"; *Virginia Quarterly Review*: "Bat House," "The Elevated," and "The Week Before She Died"; *World Literature Today*: "Daybreak" and "Parents at Rest"; and *Yale Review*: "The Middle Seat."

The following poems have appeared or will appear in the following anthologies:

Brute Neighbors: Urban Nature Poetry, Prose and Photography (DePaul, 2011): "Borders"; *City Creatures* (University of Chicago Press, 2015): "Visitations"; *Ghost Fishing: An Eco-Justice Poetry Anthology* (University of Georgia Press, 2017): "Whale Song"; *The Golden Shovel Anthology* (University of Arkansas Press, 2017): "Division Street"; *Poesia e Luce: Venezia* (Antoloia Poetica, 2016): "Of What's Sea-Locked."

"Francesca's Circle" was commissioned by Marco Nereo Rotelli for his light illumination, *Divina Natura* at The Field Museum of Chicago, June 2013.

I would like to express gratitude to my friends who have helped to encourage this work: Cynthia Atkins, Sophie Cabot Black, John Fuller, Dana Gioia, Thea Goodman, Chris Green, Susan Hahn, Joy Harjo, Grace Schulman, Jeff Shotts, and Tree Swenson.

Many thanks, also, to the incredible staff at Red Hen Press.

For my family—

Stuart, Alexandra and Stephen

Contents

III

The armored cars of dreams, contrived to let us do
so many a dangerous thing . . .

—Elizabeth Bishop, "Sleeping Standing Up"

I

Closing House

How it takes place / While someone else is eating or opening a window...
—W.H. Auden

You pack books in boxes, dismantle
library shelves

        Whitecaps after the storm; the beach
        is packed. A stretch of sand, no lifeguard.

Empty the freezer: cookie-dough
ice cream, bratwursts

        The doctor's children beg to swim.
        He answers, *No. Water's too rough.*

From tree to tree fill thistle
in goldfinch feeders

        Past the sandbar two teenage boys'
        kayak hits high waves, overturns.

Stack beach towels like cityscapes
on laundry racks

        In choppy waters the boys shout.
        Their mother on the beach cries out.

Bubble-wrap vases, lock the crystal
in dark cabinets

        Wading into the lake, the doctor
        pushes the pair back to the sandbar.

Roll down umbrellas, empty out
the kiddy pool

        But a six-footer hits, drags under.
        Current hauls him into the rip-tide.

Water impatiens, pluck tomatoes
from heavy vine

        Pediatric surgeon dies
        trying to rescue drowning boys.

Carry the last bag from the house,
load the car, drive

past Cherry Beach   No sirens. No helicopters.

    Sky ablaze. Immaculate day.

BAT HOUSE

Turn out the light and I'll explain.
—James Fenton

It's where I'm heading
It's what I overheard
The lines in the corner
The flaming word.

It's what you expected
Your greatest fear
A chip in the teacup
Bills from last year.

It's dark in the bat house
Beetles stuck on the screen
It's cold in the crawl space
Slow quarantine.

Don't lie to the drunkard
Question each doubt
Shadow the cat
Turn the light out.

If you meet me halfway
I'll tell you what for
Where it begins
Open the door.

It's the news in the paper
Same as last week
The sirens at midnight
Why you can't sleep.

The dog's in the basement
You lost the phone
The father keeps calling
Bury what's known.

Picnic Triptych

I. FROM SMALL BROWN NOTEBOOK

The tall man whose name I'd forgotten
led me down to the Roaring Fork
where he spread out a paisley blanket,
arranging chunks of cheese, baguettes,
a bottle of pale peach rosé.
A raft capsized farther upriver.
The man stood up and ran the other
direction. I waded through cold
water, saw the boaters, safe.
An uphill climb to home, I fell
asleep. Entering the house, the man
undressed, crawled next to me, his body,
a question mark. Waking, I told him
to leave. He stood, pulling on jeans,
walked across the landing just as
my husband climbed the stairs. Witnessing
the man, he turned to go. The stranger
bolted, hailing a cab outside.
My husband at the next-door bar
ordered a Glenfiddich shot.
As I approached, he motioned no.
The house alone kept quiet that night.

II. *LE DÉJEUNER SUR L'HERBE*
—Édouard Manet, 1863

He had invited her to lunch
beside the Roaring Fork, and she,
forgetting his history, said yes.

The artist had stretched a bedspread
across grass, now his empty canvas,
placing there Chianti and Brie.

Upriver a raft overturned.
He stood, brushed crumbs off his lap, mumbling,
Against the tree. Bicycle unlocked.

Trying to balance on slick rocks
to see the boaters safe on land,
she waded across slippery river.

Through gorse she climbed. Inside the stone
house she lay down on the floor, slept.
Did she dream or did he trail her

back to the house, undress, then anchor
his weight beside her? She could hear
a door slam shut. Her husband took

the stairs by twos, the dogs at his heels.

III. HALF THERE

It was a summer's day.
It was cold as winter.

He invited her down to the river,
then pretended they'd never met.

They drank beside the Roaring Fork.
Chilled, she left, without a wrap.

He shadowed her uphill.
She entered the house alone.

She didn't lock the door.
The door was locked.

On the bedroom floor she slept.
He left an imprint there.

She woke to the slam of a door.
The room was empty.

Under the wing of roof
no one spoke of this again.

The Elevated

Train on the rails
Moon buttonholes the sky
The sorrow, the sails
Your hand, my thigh.

Moon buttonholes the sky
Lines trail airplanes
Your hand, my thigh
Doors close again.

Lines trail airplanes
The lake, a ladle spoon
Doors close again
Morning. Afternoon.

The lake, a ladle spoon
Rooftops swap place
Morning, afternoon
Retrace your face.

Rooftops swap place
The sorrow, the sails
Retrace your face
Train on the rails.

STOCKHOLM SYNDROME

The husband confessed what's hard to believe.
His wife told the story, hours into night.
He spun fictions, cheated, and didn't leave.

The young son practiced a recitative.
From the car she watched, shining fierce headlights.
The husband confessed what's hard to believe.

They lived near Stockholm by the sea. Naïve,
she trusted his work-call weekends. They'd fight.
He cheated over twelve years but couldn't leave.

At a wedding, he vanished. New Year's Eve.
Bachelor brothers mixed cocktails past midnight.
The husband spun stories no one believed.

Entering the hall, he grabbed her black-knit sleeve.
A quick kiss to sharpen his appetite.
"Drinks in your cottage? Shall we leave?"

He listed each affair, said he's relieved.
Now he demands joint custody. That night
the husband confessed what she now believes.
A marriage of fractions. It's time to leave.

In need of air, she unhinged every
window, revolving ones downstairs,
upstairs skylights, mid-floor French doors,
swept into the house the salt-brine,
the cricket chirp, the osprey whistle,
the sea-current, sound of the Sound,
but had not noticed the basement
bedroom window shielded by blinds,
screen-less. Later that night when they
returned home, lights illuminating
the downstairs hall, insects inhabited
the ground floor rooms. She carried handfuls
of creatures across a River Styx—
the katydids perched on lampshades,
beach tiger beetles shuttling across
floorboards, nursery web spiders splotching
the ceiling—trying to put back
the wild fury she had released.

II

DIVISION STREET

...Prayer book and Mother, shot themselves last Sunday.
—Gwendolyn Brooks

The spire of Holy Name Cathedral rose like a prayer
above Chicago Avenue. I thumbed a leather-bound book
in catechism class, recited the *Hail Mary*. Fire and
devils blazed at night. The nuns told my mother
I had a calling. On Scott Street a man lay shot
dead in our alley. It was the Gold Coast. They prided themselves
on sidewalks safe as shrines. I questioned God, the last
to leave the room. Riots flared in Cabrini Green that Sunday.

LEAR'S WIFE

. . . if thou shouldst not be glad,
I would divorce me from thy mother's tomb,
Sepulch'ring an adult'ress.
—William Shakespeare

He faked my death,
set up this ranch
far from my three

daughters. Suburban
hell-hole. With bracelet
on ankle, house-

arrest. At noon
the bully sun
shoulders a ripe

moon. In the dark
soaps reign. The anchors
will often flash

their glitterati
weddings. Not one
daughter has birthed

the heir. In vitro—
be damned. I hose
the lawn and count

the cars like fish
slipping their shiny
chrome along asphalt.

Which sparrow missed?
Cordelia—
my gutted heart.

Seed

Upstairs in the study, watching the grey
heron steady its legs beside the pond,
I heard your message from the hospital.
You were searching for the rabbi. Outside,
beneath a magnolia tree, the children
tried to nurse a baby mouse back to life,

squeezing goat's milk from an eye dropper
and scattering seed from the everything
bagel into the corners of the shoebox.
You said this was your greatest fear.

At the burial, we were protected
from sunlight by outstretched umbrellas.
Your son said, "Daddy now is in the wind,"
and when we each threw petals and three shovels
of dirt into the grave, a gust blew strong
the blazing day. Your umbrella collapsed.

After you had called from the funeral home,
my father-in-law barked out orders
from the back porch, and all my grief,
the loss of every father, surged, uncapped.

Downstairs, in the garage, the children shout.
A hummingbird, caught between panes
of glass, batters turquoise wings against window.
We're trapped inside our awkwardness.
You cup a fluttering beat in your hands,
and the bird slips back to its sky.

SKEIN

He warned they would arrive,
web-stretching between

deck chairs and table,
harnessing limbs, loose hair.

But she couldn't hear, ignoring.
Then, she saw filigree

etched in windows, shook off
traps pulled into spun collars.

She asked, how can we stay
above board, treading water,

she asked, stepping across
flagstones from house to pond,

as if she did not know,
unraveling like threads,

strands of her clothes.

SINKHOLE

Upstairs my husband sleeps,
while downstairs on flat screen
a man tries shoveling

through a sinkhole to grasp
his brother swallowed alive
while sleeping in his bed.

My husband, pillowed under
sorrow, dreams he can save
his brother lost in water.

He reaches out his hand
to pull him from the waves
onto permanent ground

or back into the boat
where they have anchored off
the diminishing shore.

Rescuers on CNN
grab the man shoveling
spade after futile spade

of dirt, but no one reaches
the brother who has sunk
beneath the bed of earth.

OF MICE

The rhyme
repeats again:
See how they run.

See how they run.
We're victimized
by each surprise:

the farmer's wife,
the carving knife.
Don't sleep at night.

We fear

the murderers:
one captured three
towns away. Two

still free. Like mice,
they tunneled through
sewage pipes under

the penitentiary.
We lock all doors,
and, when the wind

hurtles umbrellas
against the deck,
we hide.

ACCIDENTS

We pinch the flesh of thumbs
between the corkscrew tongs:

witness a navy splotch
surface to skin, an island.

In too-high heels we catch
the step, draw blood: ten stitches.

We nick, we slice, we cut;
we bleed, we burn, we bruise.

We cloak every medallion
under sleeves, turtlenecks.

Calling for help, we fall,
fracture our wrists, our faces.

The bandages, the staples,
peeled off. The rising scars.

HEDGEROWS

Down gravelly lanes
Car-skids like thunder
Murder of hooves
Hounds chasing the prey
Study a footpath
Beagles at bay

Dark between leaves
Where thunder is cracking
Arsenal blackberries
Launch a campaign
Ignore the message
Inky terrain

Call to a driver
Why he is leaving
The house now rented
The end of a lane
Thunder like gunshots
After the rain

The light is departing
All letters illicit
Hounds keep barking
A thunder refrain
While we keep riding
Down gravelly lanes

FALLS

Rooted to outcrop
  of volcanic

rock, *penstemon,*
  saskatoon, stone

crop, ocean spray,
  upstarts anchored

to accident
  of dirt where seeds

scattered then buried,
  but now bed down,

while beneath ragged
  garden, cascade

of faith pummels
  the slate   decades

ago, spring
  flood, then mud-slide

drowned canyon walls,
  covered the dining

hall, burying
  the far-flung bridge

to the scout's camp
  beneath a cabin

a limestone grave
  quickens the heart

the kitchen clatter
  red-winged blackbirds

the flux from glacier
  lakes emptying

deliver now
  what's not to name

and strands of cotton
  skitter in air

HIGH GROUND

Across the meadow flecks
of elk congregate into the dark.

Their hooves mark the soaked hillock
rimming the pond. A garter

snake zags, slivery as lightning.
Through scrub brush a shade ripples,

crosses ancient earth mounds
where, during the *Bear Dance*, sage sprigs

once topped every stone altar.
A meteor plunges fast

as the Great Horned Owl swerves
across rooftop at sun-fall.

Along the ridge a coyote yowls,
echoed by others from all corners.

The song chills the dead, wakes the living.

BORDERS

Behind our greystone on Oakdale

a concrete landscape
covers the ground.
The alley shapes
the letter *I*.

Maneuvering
into the aisle,
I'm stuck. A neighbor
flashes headlights.

Parking is tight.
We orchestrate
our lives in such
prized real estate.

I execute
a three-point turn
into our drive.
From air what patterns

do we create
down here? Against
the back-deck's trellis
violet clematis

knots on the vine.
Will it revive?
Next door a strip
of earth which I've

witnessed transform,
despite exhaust
and lack of space,
from dirt to bloom,

continues each
spring to surprise,
illuminating
a manuscript:

the verdigris and rust outlining *I*.

THE TREE AGREEMENT

The neighbor calls the *Siberian Elm*
a "weed" tree, demands we hack
it down, says the leaves overwhelm
his property, the square backyard.

He's collar-and-tie. A weed tree?
Branches screen buildings, subway tracks,
his patch of yard. We disagree,
claim back the sap, heartwood, wild bark.

He declares the tree "hazardous."
We shelter under leaf-hoard, crossway
for squirrels, branch house for sparrows, jays.
The balcony soaks up the shade.

Chatter-song drowns out cars below.
Sun branches down. Leaves overwhelm.
The tree will stay. We tell him "no."
Root deep through pavement, *Elm*.

IMPROMPTU

When he ambles
ahead then looks
sideways to scan
the street as if
sight-reading sheet
music, I see
him several years
from now, awkward,
twelve inches taller,
stooping to clear
an overhang
of gangly branches,
and try to fix
this moment's pitch
as if fine-tuning
chords on the keys
of a piano,
how he ad-libs
his gait across
a sidewalk slab,
scattering grace notes
behind each step.

she marks her place throughout the house by the ring of her cell
phone the one she cradles in hand unaware the chime reveals
her spot one floor below where she reads on a gingham-checked
window seat knees hugged tight or sits straight-backed at the hallway
computer desk or reclines on the kitchen banquette deciphering
math puzzles the bright jangle flashes her location like highlighting
a passage in a novel as she receives cryptograms from friends *"r u
home"* *"w8 brb"* while upstairs barricaded behind a wall of books I
still shadow her trail and she like any loyal spy communicating with
allies is never alone smuggling an unknowable code

SECOND SIGHT

Green Beach, former Navy land, Vieques

Slick shale beneath our fins,
we back into the ocean,

and sink, witnessing how,
through masks, seascapes, which from

above appear as splotches—
seaweed green, moon-bleached sand—

sharpen into quick focus
(as if an ophthalmologist

had clicked a lens in place),
and we beat above the brain

coral lined up like cannonballs
where camouflaged battalions

of smallmouth grunt scatter,
then spot an ancient hawksbill

sea turtle who waves flippers
toward air, a submarine

resurfacing. The colonies
of longspine urchins seem

close up like tiny bunkers
hunkered down, poised to strike.

We peer into crevices
under the ledges, see

a handful of sergeant majors
disappear into caves.

Floating into the safety
of the shore, we shed masks

and fins. Along the beach's
south edge a sign with skull

and bones: *No Trespassing:
Explosives Under Sand.*

We weigh each step on shore.
These lines transform from pinpricks

to landmines, unpredictable,
triggered to explode.

The Middle Seat

What space can we attempt to claim
bracketed here inside a plane.
The seat-back drops: a paradox.
You're packed inside a folding box.

Each book-end stakes out territory.
Is this her armrest; whose fresh story?
Embrace your own invisible.
In fiction find a miracle.

Invent a life from something lost.
A ticket to another coast.
We land where we've lived before.
The heart darts through the open door.

III

THE WIDE STARS ABOVE OUR SKY

Class was called *The Wide Stars Above Our Sky.*
Charles and I enrolled while Shira planned
her summer abroad helping those in need.
Across the kitchen table she unfurled
a map, flattening it down with her palm,
then pointed to a small country near Russia.

Shira said, "Let's check out that hot Peruvian-
Asian restaurant downtown." I declined,
deciding to eat dinner with my parents instead.
Chai, the puppy, was eight weeks old. I plowed
through snow to purchase a knee joint at Kriser's
so she would stop chewing the chairs and table.

Shira didn't think she'd meet the right man
in the tiny country adjoining Russia.
My graduate-school poetry professor
offered the workshop every twenty minutes.
Black ice slicked down back alleys, intersections.
Monuments of snow barricaded sidewalks.

Charles transformed into my college boyfriend.
As we climbed into the blue Subaru
I forgot to explain that I already
was married. We drove miles until we reached
the summer college. My professor turned
into a high-school friend, now TV host, who ambled

around the corner of the red brick building,
counting the cumulus clouds overhead.
He wore only a blue terry-cloth bathrobe.
I asked, "Will *The Wide Stars Above Our Sky*
begin on time?" The clock said four p.m.
That was when Shira's plane took flight.

HIGH-RISE

I steer a mustard-seed Mini through snow
across the park, near the Conservatory,
the glowing flowerbeds erased by white.

Outside a building on Lakeview, I park.
The elevator man flings open doors
to a high-ceilinged, eggshell drawing room.

Mrs. Vanderbilt, in silk with beaded florets,
sits elegant in a wheelchair while guests—
dizzy in gowns, white ties—whirl around her.

The youngest in the room, I greet my parents'
long-time friends. An older man, debonair,
grazes my wrist, hands me a flute of froth.

I glimpse headlines, spread across a highboy,
dated years from now, about this man's wife,
his fourth. She outlives him into her nineties.

Across her blouse an antique necklace glints,
her husband's photo tucked inside the locket.
Her story, I realize, is my obituary.

His jacket sleeve, shiny to touch. The band
repeats "Smoke Gets in Your Eyes" as he swings
us out, pulls close. My stomach drops as if

inside the Otis elevator losing
altitude. He tries to sway me to leave
before another bell begins to ring.

New Year Poems

HALO

Walking from Christchurch toward St. Stephen's Green,
we sight the sea-glass dome of Dublin Castle.

In cobblestone courtyard, music ignites.
Gospel singers harmonize from the rampart

as iridescent balloons skid, careen.
Crossing the drawbridge, haloed creatures high

on stilts, shoulder three-jointed wings. The choir
chants "Lean on Me" while a boy climbs the fortress,

emancipates his string. The sky-shot bubble
explodes. Inside, a single flame of wings.

HOWTH

... the sun shines for you he said the day we were lying among the rhododendrons
on Howth head.
—James Joyce

When the Dart coasts into the station,
the sun illuminates the clouds.

Children balance along the wall
skirting the Clothes Repository.

From the East Promenade, a boat
ferries passengers to the Eye

of Ireland, the island where monks
once labored over every letter,

coaxing the *Garland of Howth* into bloom.

PASTURE

Powerscourt Estate Pets' Cemetery

Eugenie, Jersey Cow, died 1967,
aged 17 years, produced 17

calves and 100,000 gallons
of milk, exhales inside the heavy grave

she shares with *Princess, Aberdeen*
Angus Cow, Dublin Champion,

whose grace is cramped. She lows for air.
Tommy, Shetland Pony, hooves *Molly,*

his wife, beneath the sod, while seven
generations of *Chows* now share

a bed. Beyond the clutch of rhododendrons,
one field over, a gelding strikes a pose.

VISITATIONS
North Park Village Nature Preserve

I

They're caught off-guard
as if once shot

in black and white
blind-sided by

a flash. Mad dash
through goldenrod.

Antlers raised high
above tallgrass,

bone torches lit
to cut the path.

Could they predict
a dark outcome?

Still on the ground
two bucks, four does.

Bright intervals:
the interruption

of deer.

II

Butter-like bib
       headdress of wing

a common yellowthroat
       chattering rattle

skims across sedge
       flicks tail to shrub,

splashes and daubs
       while high above

planes scratch straight lines
       across slate.

III

Our family of four
drives past red brick buildings, one named
Dispensary, where patients,
at this once sanitarium,
were treated for TB. The strip
of park: a wall to stop disease.
Our kids, thirsty, demand chai latte.
We do not stop. At night the gates
lock deer outside, and in, swing shut
their starving. Petitions to cull
circulate. Like patients, deer wait.
Sun-up. Cattails flat against dirt:
an impression of deer.

Under Big Ben

In a mourning dream my sister-in-law,
newly widowed, arrives from Lincolnshire.
We circle round the kitchen table, each

sheltering grief, a pocket clock hidden deep,
clicking like a metronome, always off-sync.
We exchange stories, unwrapping each gift.

She says, after running errands in town,
they'd rendezvous, throughout the years, below
Big Ben. She'd ride a bike into the crescent

of his smile. Under the cast-iron bulwark
of the bell tower the chimes magnify.
They would hold tight, pose for the camera.

Against the backdrop of the wall she flashes
snapshots: their secret laughs, his auburn hair,
her rotating attire (sky-blue shift dress,

brimmed hat; dove grey seersucker and kid gloves)
while high above, outside the frame, bells stop,
the hands arrested, always six o'clock.

Whale Song

Pilot whales have a close-knit social structure that can cause them to follow sick or lost members of their pod and then resist leaving those animals.
—*Los Angeles Times*

At counters in grocery stores
friends purchase turkeys large enough
to feed twelve siblings, thirty cousins,

while our family table grows
smaller. Across the continent
the pilot whales click, call and keen

as one, then another, dry-docks.
Hovering nearby in shallow waters,
the pod can't be lured to the deep.

On linens we station pale candles,
marshal chrysanthemums in vases,
balance wedding glasses for five,

while in the graveyards the headstones
wait to be carved. Around the table:
ghost of song, empty chairs.

Ghost, Fountain

Lucia is haunted…
—Lucia di Lammermoor

water this fountain
where I am yoked

sun-break he holds
you how once I

this secret dark
dagger my body

rip off the collar
your cage don't wait

my neck his breath
these woods this water

my waist his ring
his grip blood sister

LABYRINTH

The night, music and stars began to play a role in my painting.
—Joan Miro

While the *Luftwaffe* dropped bombs at night,
you brushed and rubbed *The Constellations*
across a pad, sketching the scales of birds.

In the marriage bed your lunar bird,
Pilar, tossed under the constellation
of her hair, climbing ladders into night.

This pine-tree hillside: your canvas, a night
of quavers and clefs. A thread unspooled by the *Sunbird*,
a girl, connects the runes of your constellations.

Drama Drama

Outside our bedroom, actors cluster
on a terrace rehearsing cues.

Garbed in Renaissance gowns, the players
recite their lines in iambs, trochees.

A couple sleeps under the balustrade.
From the tower a crimson banner drops.

Our family cracks open its own stage
while thieves steal loaves of day-old bread.

* * *

Stuart and I catch a ride
to watch more plays in the Loop. We're backseat
driving. In front: two producers, beside
an aging actress, sit straight like eggs in a carton.

The star says, "Stop
at that diner, *Salt 'n Pepper.*" She demands
the car exits Lake Shore Drive. We question,
when can we bolt to catch the Brown Line
back to Wellington?

Stripes through slats wake us up.
A pair, stage right, enters. Stephen raids
the bed while Alexandra, nonchalant,
stands framed inside the bedroom door.

The Marriage Bed

Dream Caused by the Flight of a Bee around a Pomegranate a Second before Awakening
—Salvador Dali

That he painted her suspended above a rock—his wife,
asleep, naked, after biting a pomegranate, seeds spit
into ocean. That the bee, before a sting, craves the sweet
suck and sip of Venus-fruit. That the artist, straight-backed
in bony armchair, would doze, heavy key between thumb
and forefinger. That the clatter of metal hitting the tin plate beneath
his hand, wakes him up: a Capuchin monk technique. That she
does not tumble into the sea, his muse, afloat, scumbled there.
But when Miro pictures his wife in *Woman Dreaming*
of Escape, one eye is open wide while a ladder hovers, cross-hatched,
above her head. That this wife has no exit. That the orb
disgorges the red snapper which spews out two
tigers with bayonet about to jab the under-flesh
of her arm. That I forgot to mention the elephant on spider-stilts
balancing an obelisk on back. The artist etched the sky
by noon, the backdrop after six p.m. That in the Thyssen,
when I was late, racing past Picasso and Chagall,
Dali bellowed, arresting my step. I lost
sight of my husband on the mezzanine. That Gala
is stung. That Pilar takes flight. That sleeping
women interrupt their spouses' canvases.

IV

DAYBREAK

After the watch, *dorveille*,
pin-prick of stud in sky,
before that six a.m.
first warbler wake-up call
from elm above the deck,
in dream a wife no longer
answers to her name, entering
chapters of houses, rooms
of light, keys to be clicked
in every door while outside
rise banks of wildflowers
she'll climb.

FRANCESCA'S CIRCLE

Here, there, down, up, they swirl, again, again;
No hope comforts them ever, no,
Not even hope of stillness, but of blunted pain.
—Dante Alighieri

Paolo my collar   swallow this pit
my husband's brother   I spit you out
forged in hellfire   brother   lodestar
we spin and torque   my lover   husband's
our wrists like thorns   out of reach   my hell
cutting one pulse   spiraling cavern
forearm apart   such wind the blast
I cannot bite   scorches your words
my tongue this fire

CLOISTER

The armor of the books
The amen of the desk

The Geography of the Heavens
Mapped against the walls.

The orchard of the carpet
The ladder of the shelves

The window of the sparrow
Illuminates this shell.

Shifting Ground

I. HIGH TIDE, MID-MARRIAGE

The streak   of sun
            through slat.   The slap

of brine.   Sharp mollusks
            dug deep.   How love

stays calm.   The plates,
            hunkering   through storm,

stacked up.   How water
            rises   to fill

the tureen   of bay
            to brim.   The queen

and knight   squared off.
            Slow draw.   This palm,

in yours,   will cup
            a sea   or salt,

shell welded   to sand.
            How sun   arcs, crowns:

dashed gem-   stone sheet,
            bracelet   of wave.

II. STILT COTTAGE, LOW TIDE

Where the leopard shark's two-
chambered heart hammers,
neighboring skeins of brant geese

doze on the gray-sheet slate,
the punctuated white
of their tails flick the sun,

citizens of the sheen
floating, while the stockbrokers
dial quick calls and the judges

elsewhere pummel their gavels.
In eel grass herring eggs
quiver. A newscaster

announces: *Reindeer herders
stumble upon colossal
craters in permafrost.*

Our cottage, cantilevered
above a strike-slip fault,
hovers above the estuary.

I watch a lone brant dive
where shells lie open, cracked.
This tendency to drift.

RIDDLE

SKYLIGHT ABOVE

            the bed where sun

and moon swap

            you chart the arc

hours   the deck

            the window   pulse

or surf   a clock

OF WHAT'S SEA-LOCKED

                                        inside ink-dark

that sweet secretes

                                          covert and whorl

nacre of shell

                                          beyond the flume

the shade-backed hump

                                          oh Inverness

elsewhere you toss

                                          that darker half

as moon slips into

Behind the Slant

                                        choirs of sparrows

in oak branches

                                        try to pry

the jet from stone

                                        crime with no

confession padlock

                                        bereft of that

miniscule

                                        key   the jetty

loose and untethered

                                        this sorrow

though overgrown

My Mother Descends

After he died, she slipped away,
visiting her husband, my father,
every night, in the underworld.

At dinner she hides spoons inside
her sleeves. After sunset she crosses
the River Styx, braving storm-torn waves.

Rehearsing death, she lies in bed
for twelve-hour stints. The skiff, so fragile,
shakes when she recovers her balance.

When she descends to bring him back,
clouds skim her eyes. She cannot see,
catching only glints of his silver hair.

There's never enough cutlery
for Charon. Cerberus snarls hot.
What she wouldn't give to convince Hades.

Awake at sunrise, her limbs, heavy,
ache from the labor. She is weary
and observes silence with the living.

THE WEEK BEFORE SHE DIED

I dream us young, again,
mother and daughter back
on 69th Street inside
our old brownstone—across
from the church, patch of lawn—

a house neglected, wrecked,
as if the family
had been forced at gunpoint
to move away. In corners
dirt stacked like miniscule

anthills; along the edges
of room—crumpled clothes, bodiless;
littered across the floor
dry-cleaning bags, vestiges
of what they once protected.

A Turkish scarf, embroidered
with sequins, glitter, beads,
tantalizes. My mother
holds it close, says, "You should
wear it." The doorbell rings.

At the top of the stairs
he waits for us to answer.
My mother's ballet partner,
Russian, stows something covert
behind his almond eyes. With three

regal strides he commands
our gaze, pronounces the red
brocade robe his, lofts high
the scarf, the sash he flung
in *Giselle*, circling the empty

living room. With mischief he bows
low before my mother. Her love
for him, a mountain. The doorbell
chimes. A blond, blue-eyed dancer,
in epaulets, arrives.

She straightens shoulders, turns,
walks away. Rudy asks
Erik, "Did you ever tell her
about us?" No response. The secrets
men keep, my mother knows.

PARENTS AT REST

They would sit quietly as something dense
and radiant swirled around them . . .
—B.H. Fairchild

How, in the afternoon,
after performing chores
in sync—grocery shopping,
his cooking, her cleaning up—
they would lie on the angled couch,
toe-to-toe, his side, hers,
books in hand, his biographies,
her murder mysteries,
listening to Beethoven.
He'd nod off while she read
to the rhythm of his breath.
Outside the open windows
waves thumped on stony beach,
seagulls buffeting wind.

The houses of their birth,
both yellow brick, now crumbled:
one perched hilltop above
pasture, the other, prairie-school
city house with sunken garden.
How he waited for her
these many years in the graveyard
below her childhood home
where now they sleep together
beneath the rhapsody
of meadowsweet.

Haiku

I entered the room
of this life to discover
time had come to move.

Feathers and snow sail
from sky. On the balcony
heart saddle, claw, wing.

Marked now for decades
we're palmed a day-bright penny.
Glaciers thumb the sand.

END OF DAY

Arc of the goldfinch
glint across the spring-fed pond
a surprise of light

NOTES

"Seed" is dedicated to Julie Parson-Nesbitt; "Falls" to Debra Gwartney: "High Ground" to Daryl Hannah; *"Impromptu"* to Stephen Brainerd; "text" to Alexandra Brainerd; "Under Big Ben" to Claire Brainerd; *"Riddle"* after Laura Kasischke.

"Closing House"
    Epigraph is from W.H. Auden's "Musée des Beaux Arts."

"Bat House"
    Epigraph is from James Fenton's "I'll Explain."

"Division Street"
    Epigraph is from Gwendolyn Brooks' "A Man of the Middle Class."

"Lear's Wife"
    Epigraph is from William Shakespeare's *King Lear*, Act II, scene 2.

"Howth"
    Epigraph is from James Joyce's *Ulysses*, chapter 18.

"Ghost, Fountain"
    Epigraph is from Gaetano Donizetti's *Lucia Di Lammermoor*, Act I, scene 2.

"Francesca's Circle"
    Epigraph comes from my translation of Dante Alighieri's Canto 5, *Inferno.*

"Parents at Rest"
    Epigraph is from B.H. Fairchild's "The Dumka."

BIOGRAPHICAL NOTE

Elise Paschen is the author of *Bestiary, Infidelities* (winner of the Nicholas Roerich Poetry Prize), and *Houses: Coasts*. As an undergraduate at Harvard, she received the Garrison Medal for poetry. She holds M.Phil. and D.Phil. degrees from Oxford University. Her poems have been published in *The New Yorker* and *Poetry Magazine*, among other magazines, and in numerous anthologies. She is the editor of *The New York Times* best-selling anthology *Poetry Speaks to Children* and co-editor of *Poetry Speaks* and *Poetry in Motion*, among other anthologies. She is a member of the Osage Nation. Former Executive Director of the Poetry Society of America, she is a co-founder of *Poetry in Motion*, a nationwide program that places poetry posters in subway cars and buses. Paschen teaches in the MFA Writing Program at the School of the Art Institute and lives in Chicago with her husband and their two children.

CPSIA information can be obtained
at www.ICGtesting.com
Printed in the USA
BVOW08s1307090617

486507BV00002B/12/P